Golden threads

by
Selwyn Hughes

Further study section compiled by
Trevor J. Partridge

CWR

© Selwyn Hughes 1987

Material originally published in Every Day With Jesus in 1982 and 1984

ISBN 1 85345 004 9

**CWR, 10 Brooklands Close, Windmill Road,
Sunbury-on-Thames, Middx TW16 7DX**
Illustrations by Norman Savine
Cover photo: Ace Photo Agency/Laszlo Willinger
Typeset by Creative Editors & Writers Ltd, Watford
Printed by Crusade Printing, Chertsey

DAY 1

Golden threads
MATTHEW 5:38–48

"...He causes his sun to rise on the evil and the good, and sends rain on the righteous and the unrighteous." (v. 45: NIV)

Through her long life of faithful service to the Lord, Corrie ten Boom experienced many afflictions and learned to allow God to work through them. She learned to receive the grace He poured out at such times and knew Him to be sovereign. This knowledge of her heavenly Father is reflected in a poem she quoted:

> "My life is but a weaving, between my God and me.
> I do not choose the colours, he worketh steadily.
> Ofttimes he weaveth sorrow, and I in foolish pride,
> Forget he sees the upper, and I the underside.
>
> Not till the loom is silent and the shuttles cease to fly,
> Will God unroll the canvas and explain the reason why.
> The dark threads are as needful in the skilful Weaver's hand,
> As the threads of gold and silver in the pattern he has planned."

What a difference our attitude to those dark threads makes! We need not be fearful and try to avoid these times of trial, to walk away from unhappy home circumstances or financial disaster; to rely on temporary answers to stress when we have the divine answer to the dark threads because the Weaver loves us with a perfect love.

During the next four weeks we are going to look at some areas in which many find dark threads woven into the tapestry of life. We will learn that Christians are not exempt from the natural laws that govern the universe — we may through grace be able to overcome them, but we are not able to avoid them. God will only weave dark threads if He can turn them to good effect — He only allows what He can use.

PRAYER: Father, thank You for reminding me that even though I am a Christian, I am still governed by natural laws that apply equally to everyone. I cannot be exempt, but through You I can overcome. I am so grateful. Amen.

FURTHER STUDY: Jas. 2:14–26; 1 Tim. 4:9–16; 2 Tim. 2:15
1 *What is James teaching us?* 2 *How does Paul apply this to Timothy?*

DAY 2

Unhappy home circumstances
1 PETER 3:1–12

"...heirs together of the grace of life..." (v. 7)

An area in which many people find dark threads is that of the home. Remember, the Weaver is skilful and will weave grace in the dark threads of *unhappy home circumstances*. It may be that you have an unhappy marriage, or a bad relationship with your parents. Perhaps you are a parent whose teenage children are becoming rebellious, and causing you deep concern. You can find grace amongst the dark threads.

What is to be done? First go over the whole matter anew. See if some of the reasons for your unhappy home circumstances are not in you. Be objective and relentless with yourself. Remember, grace flows to help you live with a problem, but if *you* are the problem, then it's not grace you need, but courage to face up to it. If, in looking at yourself, you find things that need putting right, then confess this to God and to those whom you may have hurt. Leave it to others to confess their faults. Don't try and confess another person's sins. When you have done this, then you can sit back and relax, for you are in a position to receive the grace that God provides for such situations.

I know many Christians who are caught in the threads of unhappy home circumstances, and I observe them day by day doing what the oyster does when it gets an irritating grain of sand in its shell — it forms a pearl around the irritation. Whenever you are unable to get free of a situation, then God gives grace to enable you to throw 'the pearl of character' around the problem. The problem, then, becomes a trysting place where daily you and the Lord work out life together in spite of the irritation. No matter how difficult the problem, how unhappy the circumstances, how depressing the situation, you can find grace. Not just today, but every day!

PRAYER: O God my Father, I come to You with the tapestry of my life. I know, when I can't get out of a dungeon, that I am not blocked, for I can make my circumstances make me. Help me to avail myself of Your grace whatever the pattern. For Jesus' sake. Amen.

FURTHER STUDY: Psa. 127:1–5; Gen. Ch. 4; Matt. 5:23–24
1 *What was the problem of the first home?* 2 *What was Jesus' solution?*

DAY 3

Don't correct by disapproval
MATTHEW 7:1–5

"For you will be judged by the way you criticise others…"
(v. 2: J.B. Phillips)

Today we begin asking ourselves a pertinent question: How does God's grace enable us to live securely in the midst of unhappy home circumstances? Well, for one thing, it enables us to cope with the situation without resorting to nagging complaints. Remember the Pharisees in the New Testament? They thought the only way to change people was by showing disapproval. They tried it, and only ended in being disapproved of themselves. Once they journeyed all the way from Jerusalem to Galilee, and what did they see? The astonishing miracles of God's only begotten Son? The gates of life being thrown open to stricken souls? Oh, no! They saw only the fact that the disciples ate with unwashed hands. They overlooked the tremendous and saw only the trivial. They belittled themselves by what they saw.

Attempting to correct others by nagging complaints is a failure — and always will be. The offending person reacts by justifying their action. They say, "Look how unloving and misunderstanding my family are. I'm justified in finding love and understanding somewhere else." The Pharisees tried to correct the world by disapproving of it, but it didn't work. The one who is hypercritical usually turns out to be hypocritical too.

There are two ways to get rid of a block of ice. One is to try to smash it with a hammer, in which case you only succeed in shattering it; the other way is to melt it, in which case you really do get rid of it. God's grace, flowing into an unhappy home situation, is there to enable you, not to smash the situation, but to melt it. The way of the Pharisees is not the Christian way; the Christian way is the way of grace. And grace, like love, never fails.

PRAYER: O Father, help me to see that the way of disapproval — the way of the Pharisees — is not a way that works. Enable me to use Your grace and power to take the Christian way in everything — the way of caring. For Jesus' sake. Amen.

FURTHER STUDY: Ex. 15:20–16:3; Deut. 1:19–35; Jn. 6:43; 1 Cor. 10:10; Phil. 2:14
1 *Why did the children of Israel murmur?* 2 *What fruit did these seeds bring?*

DAY 4

Compliments change things
LEVITICUS 19:1–18

"Do not seek revenge or bear a grudge ... but love..."
(v. 18: NIV)

We continue examining the importance of being gracious and showing love in the midst of unhappy home circumstances. Another thing that grace enables us to do in the midst of difficult relationships in the home is to give sincere and genuine compliments to the other members of the family. If I have learned one thing in my years of counselling families who are in trouble, it is this — compliments, sincere compliments, have the power to transform human relationships. A famous psychologist said in my presence, "I have never counselled anyone with serious emotional problems who can remember being complimented by his parents." Can you see what he meant? Every emotionally ill-adjusted person he had counselled couldn't remember ever being complimented.

Compliments are to the personality what food is to the body. You must have heard of the Sunday school teacher who, upon asking a new Sunday school scholar for his full name, was told, "I'm Johnny Don't." "Are you sure that's your full name?" queried the teacher. "Well, that's what my mother and father call me when I'm at home," was his reply. Poor Johnny must have responded to that with an attitude of inner resistance and rebellion. It reminds me of the boy who said, "My father told me to sit down, but I was still standing up on the inside."

Take this example, however. A little boy sat down at the table and began to eat before his parents had said grace. When gently reprimanded by them, he said, "Well anyway, I didn't chew." His wise mother and father complimented him for that much restraint! Then they appealed for full restraint. Bring into the home genuine compliments and appreciation, and the hearts of all in it will open up to their genial warmth.

PRAYER: O Father, help me to compliment people sincerely, especially my family, and when I can't appreciate them for what they are, help me to appreciate them for what they can be. Amen.

FURTHER STUDY: Rev. 2:1–7; 2 Tim. 4:8; Matt. 25:23; 1 Pet. 5:4
1 *How did the Lord deal with the church at Ephesus?* 2 *What was the response to the faithful servant?*

DAY 5

"Prompted by her mother"
DEUTERONOMY 6:1–12

"These commandments that I give you today are to be upon your hearts. Impress them on your children…" (vv. 6–7: NIV)

It is a well-known fact that children in a home catch the attitudes of their parents rather than their words. The child is much like the subconscious mind — he learns by what he sees people acting on, rather than by what they say. The account concerning the daughter of Herodias dancing before Herod, reads: "Prompted by her mother, she said, 'Give me…'" (Matt. 14:8, NIV). What did the daughter want? She wanted what her mother wanted — the head of John the Baptist.

Some people wonder at the undisciplined youth of this generation. I don't. We have only to look back over the previous generation and we have the answer. This generation has been 'prompted' by the parents of today. Those who express surprise at the state of affairs amongst modern-day youth say, "We told our children of the importance of morality and religion; why didn't they listen?" Well, perhaps it's because this generation of parents repeated the sanctions of morality and religion with less conviction and example. The generation before today's parents, having undergone a wave of evangelical awakening at the end of the last century and the beginning of this, had some deep convictions. The next generation lived on the afterglow of that, but with little *personal* experience.

A child learns not so much from what parents say, but from what they do; and if parents contradict, by their own actions and attitudes, what they say, the child structures himself on what they do. The influence of actions and attitudes is far more powerful than words. The prodigal son came back because he had a good father. The prodigal daughter (the daughter of Herodias) never came back because she had a bad mother.

PRAYER: O God, help Your Church to bring into the home such a flame of pure living that the young might be supplied with a torch that will never go out. In Jesus' Name I pray. Amen.

FURTHER STUDY: 1 Sam. Ch. 2; Prov. 22:6; 2 Cor. 12:14; Eph. 6:4
1 *Who did God hold responsible for sin in the temple?* 2 *What is the Biblical principle?*

DAY 6

Facing an affair
HEBREWS 12:1–15

"Be careful that none of you fails to respond to the grace of God, for if he does there can spring up in him a bitter spirit…" (v. 15: J.B. Phillips)

At this point in my writing I received a letter from a distressed woman who said, "My home is breaking up due to my husband's affair with another woman. What can I do?"

How do we maintain spiritual poise when a partner is involved in an affair? I feel compelled to share a précis of my answer to this dear woman with you.

Firstly, remind yourself that there is grace even in this dark part of the tapestry. Throw yourself on God. Others have received grace to face this problem — and so can you. Secondly, ask yourself: "Why did it happen?" Often (not always) an affair begins out of the desire for companionship and love which is not found in the home. If there is a deficiency here, recognise it and decide what can be done to correct it. Thirdly, face any anger you might feel and don't repress it. While the Bible exhorts us not to express anger, it is not wrong to acknowledge it. If you are angry, admit it to yourself, and ask God to help you deal with it. Fourthly, confess your deficiencies to your partner, not for the purpose of winning them back, but because it is right. Confess your own faults, and never confess your partner's — that is fatal. Let your partner confess their own if they wish. Fifthly, don't alternate between tongue-lashing and fawning over your partner. No one is corrected by nagging — no one. Some who find that nagging doesn't work then turn to an affectation of devotion and love. They overdo it, and it comes across as a device to win back the partner. It defeats itself. Sixthly, keep believing in your partner in spite of their actions. The very belief will create the thing you believe in. And lastly, lift up your partner in constant prayer. Affairs are often temporary; they grow fast and can wither fast. Prayer can help dissolve them.

PRAYER: O God, I am so thankful that You have an answer to every problem. For this, and every other problem, help me to affirm always: God is my answer. For Jesus' sake. Amen.

FURTHER STUDY: Jn. 8:1–11; Psa. 78:38; Col. 2:13
1 *How did the Pharisees respond to the woman?* 2 *How did Jesus respond?*

DAY 7

Our three primary needs
COLOSSIANS 2:1–10

"...in Him you have been made complete..." (v. 10: RAV)

A further principle we must learn if we are to accept the grace poured out when we experience unhappy home circumstances is: *depend on God, and not on anyone else, to meet the deepest needs of your personality.* Allow this truth to take hold of your innermost being and, I promise you, you will become a transformed person.

The needs of our personality can be categorised in a number of ways, but the most basic ones are these: (1) the need to be loved unconditionally (security); (2) the need to be valued (self-worth) and (3) the need to make a meaningful contribution to God's world (significance). Human beings can only function effectively to the degree that these needs are met. If they are unsatisfied, our ability to function as a person is greatly hindered; if they are adequately met, then, other things being equal, we have the potential of functioning effectively.

Notice, however, this important point — our needs for security, significance and self-worth can be *fully* met only in a close and ongoing relationship with the Lord Jesus Christ. If we do not let Christ meet those needs, then because they have to be met in order for us to function effectively, we will attempt to get them met in and through others. Although many do not realise it, this is what draws many people toward marriage, because they see the possibility of having their needs met through their partner. But no human being, however loving, kind and considerate they may be, can fully meet these needs. I say again: they can be met fully only in a close and ongoing relationship with the Lord Jesus Christ.

PRAYER: Father, I sense that I am on the verge of something big and challenging. Help me to grasp this, for I sense that if I do, I shall become a transformed person. In Jesus' Name I ask it. Amen.

FURTHER STUDY: Eph. Chs. 1 & 2
1 *Where is Christ?* 2 *Where are we?*

DAY 8

Are you a manipulator?
JOHN 15:9–17

"My command is this: Love each other as I have loved you." (v. 12: NIV)

Yesterday we touched on what is perhaps the biggest single problem in marital unhappiness — trying to get one's partner to meet needs that can only be fully met through a relationship with Jesus Christ. This issue is so important that I propose to spend another day discussing it.

What happens if we do not allow God to meet our basic needs? We will try to get those needs met in some other way. *Some people try to find satisfaction in achievement or work.* This, however, fails to bring lasting satisfaction, and whenever their inner discomfort reaches the threshold of awareness, they anaesthetise it with more activities, more achievement and more work.

Another way, as we have already said, is *to attempt to get these needs met in marriage.* Can you see the problem this produces? If we enter marriage as a way of getting our needs met, then we consciously or unconsciously become involved in manipulating our partner to meet our needs. Instead of following the Christian vision of marriage, which is to minister to our partners from a position of security in Christ's love, we begin to manipulate them to meet our needs. Thousands of marriages, perhaps millions, are caught up in this treadmill — each trying to get their partner to meet the needs that only God can fully meet. The best way to get our needs met is to depend on God to meet them. When we lock into Him and focus on how much He loves and values us, and on His purpose for our lives, then and only then are we free to minister in the way He prescribes in His Word. Without that inner security, we become exposed and vulnerable to the likes or dislikes of our partner. We become puppets — not people.

PRAYER: O my Lord and Master, take me in Your arms today and make me so conscious of Your love that I will no longer manipulate others to love me, but minister to them with the love I already have. For Jesus' sake I ask it. Amen.

FURTHER STUDY: 1 Cor. Ch. 13; Rom. 5:8, 8:35; 1 Jn. 3:16
1 *List 15 qualities of love.* 2 *Is their emphasis on giving or getting?*

DAY 9

Making God more meaningful
1 JOHN 4:7–21

"No-one has ever seen God; but if we love each other, God lives in us and his love is made complete in us." (v. 12: NIV)

We have been seeing over the past two days that a vital principle to follow to receive the grace that God longs to give us during times of trouble in the home is to depend on the Lord to meet our basic needs. You might ask yourself: if the Lord can meet my needs for security, self-worth and significance, why do I need a human partner at all?

The answer to that question flows out of the next principle: *in the relationship with your partner or your children, focus more on what you can give than what you can get.* Now this can be exceedingly difficult, of course, if you are not allowing God to meet your needs, but once you are secure in Him, *everything He asks you to do becomes possible.* Assuming our needs for security, significance and self-worth are being met in God, we are then in a position to fulfil God's true purpose for marriage, which is this: God, who is an invisible, intangible, eternal Being, has designed marriage to be a visible, tangible demonstration of the reality of His love as we minister love and consideration to one another.

Just think of it — in marriage we have the marvellous privilege of demonstrating God's love to our partners in a way that they can feel, touch and understand. Our love will not add to the *fact* of their security in Christ, but it will add to the degree to which they *feel* it. No wonder Martin Luther said that marriage was the greatest way God had of teaching us the truths about Himself. And the second greatest way? You've got it! The Church!

PRAYER: Father, to realise that I have the privilege of bringing the reality of Your love to others, and thus making You more real to them, is so incredible that it almost blows my mind! But I know it is true. Make me worthy of this privilege. For Jesus' sake. Amen.

FURTHER STUDY· Matt. 10:1–8; Lk. 6:38; Prov. 11:25; Acts 20:35; 2 Cor. 9:6
1 *What did Jesus teach His disciples?* 2 *How can you demonstrate this today?*

DAY 10

A check-up for husbands
EPHESIANS 5:22–33

"Husbands, love your wives, just as Christ loved the church…" (v. 25: NIV)

Over the next two days I want to establish two final principles for dealing with troubles in the home: one for the husbands and one for the wives. Today we begin with the men: *be prepared to give yourself a spiritual check-up on how you are doing as a husband.* Cross out whichever answer does *not* apply.

1. Do you still 'court' your wife with an unexpected gift of flowers or chocolates? (Anniversaries and birthdays not to be included) (YES/NO)

2. Are you careful never to criticise her in front of others? (YES/NO)

3. Do you make an effort to understand her varying feminine moods and help her through them? (YES/NO)

4. Do you depend on your wife to meet your basic personal needs? (YES/NO)

5. Do you pray together? (YES/NO)

6. Do you share at least half your recreation time with your wife and family? (YES/NO)

7. Are you alert for opportunities to praise and compliment her? (YES/NO)

8. Do you go to church together? (YES/NO)

9. Is she first in your life — after the Lord? (YES/NO)

10. Have you forgiven her for any hurts or problems she may have caused you? (YES/NO)

A score of 7 to 10 'yes's' — excellent! Below 7 'yes's' — you've got some work ahead of you.

PRAYER: Father, You who have set us in families, help me to be the person You intend me to be, both in my marriage and in my home. This I ask in Jesus' Name. Amen.

FURTHER STUDY: Eccl. 9:1–9; Gen. 2:23–24; Col. 3:18–21; 1 Pet. 3:7
1 *What does the word 'cleave' mean?* 2 *Why are our prayers often hindered?*

DAY 11

A check-up for wives
1 PETER 3:1–12

"Wives, in the same way be submissive to your husbands…" (v. 1: NIV)

Yesterday the men were asked to examine themselves, using a simple questionnaire, as to how they were doing as husbands. Today a similar opportunity is extended to wives.

1. Are you depending on the Lord to meet your basic needs for security, significance and self-worth? (YES/NO)

2. Can you meet financial reverses bravely without condemning your husband for his mistakes, or comparing him unfavourably with others? (YES/NO)

3. Do you dress with an eye for your husband's likes and dislikes in colour and style? (YES/NO)

4. Do you keep up your own personal prayer life so that you may meet everything that arises with poise? (YES/NO)

5. Do you avoid daydreaming or fantasising about other men you might have married? (YES/NO)

6. Are you sensitive to your husband's moods and feelings and know when and when not to bring up delicate issues? (YES/NO)

7. Do you respect your husband? (YES/NO)

8. Are you careful never to criticise your husband in front of others? (YES/NO)

9. Do you keep track of the day's news and what is happening in the world so that you can discuss these with your husband? (YES/NO)

10. Are you a 'submissive' wife? (YES/NO)

A score of 7 to 10 'yes's' — excellent. Below 7 'yes's' — it's decision time.

PRAYER: My heavenly Father, I realise the tender relationships of home can be a shrine, or they can be a snarl. Keep my inner shrine from all wrong attitudes and from all worry. Let me approach today's challenge in the knowledge that "I can do all things through Christ who strengthens me". Amen.

FURTHER STUDY: Prov. 31:10–31; 1 Tim. 3:11; Esth. 1:20
1 *What are the characteristics of a virtuous woman?* 2 *What do her children call her?*

DAY 12

When broken by stress
PSALM 71:1–24

"You have let me sink down deep in desperate problems. But you will bring me back to life again up from the depths of the earth." (v. 20: TLB)

Now we turn to examine together another major area of dark threads in life — *stress*. Often I get letters from people saying something like this: "I feel I am on the verge of a breakdown. No one thing seems to be responsible for it, but I just can't cope. My doctor says I am suffering from stress. Can the Bible meet this need?" I am bold to say that it can. God can take a person overcome by stress, and build into their lives insights and principles which will enable them to live above and beyond its paralysing grip.

We ask ourselves: what exactly is 'stress'? One doctor defines it as "wear and tear on the personality which, if uncorrected, can result in a physical or mental breakdown". Donald Norfolk, a British osteopath who has made a special study of stress, claims that it comes from two main causes: (1) too little change, or (2) too much change. He says that to function at peak efficiency, we all need a certain amount of novelty and change. However, when changes come *too fast* for us to cope with, the personality is put under tremendous stress.

Dr Thomas H. Holmes, a recognised authority on the subject of stress, measures stress in terms of 'units of change'. For example, the death of a loved one measures 100 units, divorce 73 units, pregnancy 40 units, moving or altering a home 25 units and Christmas 12 units. His conclusion is that no one can handle more than 300 units of stress in a twelve-month period without suffering physically or emotionally during the next two years. Holmes, of course, was speaking from a strictly human point of view — with God 'all things are possible'.

PRAYER: Father, You have taught me much on how to turn my weaknesses into strengths. Teach me now how to handle stress. I cannot change my surroundings — but I can change my attitude. Help me to do this. For Jesus' sake. Amen.

FURTHER STUDY: Lk. 10:38–42; Phil. 4:6; Psa. 127:2; Matt. 6:25
1 *What was Jesus' response to Martha?* 2 *How did it differ from His response to Mary?*

DAY 13

Find the cause — find the cure
PSALM 139:1–24

"Search me, O God, and know my heart; test me and know my anxious thoughts." (v. 23: NIV)

Were you surprised to discover yesterday that Christmas earned 12 points on Dr Thomas Holmes' stress scale? Let me tell you that in the week leading up to Christmas, there are more suicides and breakdowns than in any other week of the year. This is because the gaiety and festivity of the Christmas season stands out in such marked contrast to the melancholy feelings of the depressed that they are easily pushed over the edge into suicide or a breakdown.

What then is the first step toward recovery from, or prevention of, stress? This: *identify what causes you to feel stress.* No two people react to stress in quite the same way. One person may revel in frequent change, while another may be thrown into a state of disquiet if a piece of furniture is moved around in a room. Dr Hans Selye, a world-famous expert on stress, says: "The mere fact of knowing what hurts has a curative value." Get alone in the presence of God with a pen and a sheet of paper, and ask the Lord to help you identify the causes of your stress.

You can help prime the pump of questioning by asking yourself the following: What one thing above all others makes me jumpy and irritable, or gives me the feeling I can't cope? (That could be stress factor No. 1) How do I react to change? Easily, or with difficulty? How much competition can I take? Keep on questioning yourself until you pin down the things that produce stress in your system. It is only when you establish the origins of stress in your life that you can set about the task of building up Biblical principles that will not only modify its impact, but enable you to turn your weaknesses into strengths.

PRAYER: Father, teach me how to respond to life so that, instead of a breakdown, I may experience a breakthrough — a breakthrough into a new way of living. For Jesus' sake. Amen.

FURTHER STUDY: Mk. 4:35–41; 1 Pet. 5:7; Matt. 13:22; Lk. 12:29
1 *Why were the disciples full of stress when Jesus was not?* 2 *How did Jesus respond?*

DAY 14

What a waste!
PHILIPPIANS 4:1–13

"Do not be anxious about anything, but in everything, by prayer and petition, with thanksgiving, present your requests to God." (v. 6: NIV)

We continue meditating on the principles we can use when our lives are threatened by stress: *recognise the symptoms of stress*. No alarm bells ring in our homes or offices when we are suffering undue stress, but there are adequate warning signs. People under stress generally become irritable and over-react to relatively trivial frustrations. They show a change in their sleep patterns, and become increasingly tired and restless. They derive less pleasure from life, experience no joy while praying or reading the Bible, laugh less and become plagued with feelings of inadequacy and self-doubt. They sometimes develop psychosomatic complaints such as tension headaches, indigestion and other things.

Some people have what is known as 'target organs' — physical organs that are the first to suffer when they are under stress. Harold Wilson confessed that whenever he had to fire a colleague, he suffered acute stomach pains. Henry Ford suffered cramps in his stomach whenever he had to make an important business decision. Trotsky, when under pressure, used to develop bouts of high temperature, and frequently had to spend time in the Crimea recuperating. One businessman I know always has a glass of milk on his desk from which he takes frequent sips in order to calm his nagging peptic ulcer.

Are you able to recognise your own particular patterns of stress? You owe it to God and yourself to find out. The waste that goes on in Christian circles through believers channelling their energies into coping with stress, rather than in extending the Kingdom of God, is appalling.

PRAYER: O God, sharpen my ability to recognise the things I do that contribute to stress in my life, so that all my energies can be channelled into spiritual activity, not self-activity. For Jesus' sake. Amen.

FURTHER STUDY: Lk. 12:15–34; 2 Tim. 1:12; 2 Cor. 11:22–33, 12:7–10
1 *What was the key to Paul's trust under stress?* 2 *List six reasons Jesus gave for not worrying about tomorrow.*

DAY 15

Stop and smell the roses
MATTHEW 6:25–34

"...Consider the lilies of the field, how they grow..." (v. 28: RSV)

Another principle that helps us cope with stress is this: *seek to overcome any rigidity in your personality*. You can best understand 'rigidity' by comparing it with its opposite — flexibility. A more formal definition of 'rigidity' is this: "The inability or refusal to change one's actions or attitudes even though objective conditions indicate that a change is desirable."

The rigid person clings to certain ways of thinking and acting, even when they are injurious to the personality and burn up their emotional energy. Someone described it as similar to driving a car with the brakes on. Take the housewife who worries herself into a migraine attack because she cannot maintain a scrupulously tidy home while her grandchildren are visiting. Or the businessman who triggers off another gastric ulcer because he falls behind with his schedule when his secretary is away sick.

Inflexible goals can be crippling fetters. It's no good saying, "But there are things that have to be done, and if I don't do them, they just won't get done." Perhaps you need to rearrange your priorities, adjust your lifestyle and learn to say 'no'. As someone put it, "We must not drive so relentlessly forward that we cannot stop and smell the roses by the wayside." You may be caught up in the midst of one of the busiest weeks of the year, but pause for a moment and ask yourself: am I driving, or am I *being driven*? Am I in control of my personality, or is it in control of me? Today, decide to take a step away from rigidity by pausing to "smell a rose".

PRAYER: O God, I am now at grips with the raw material of living: out of it must come a person — Your person. Help me to be rigid only in relation to You, and flexible about everything else. For Jesus' sake. Amen.

FURTHER STUDY: Gen. Ch. 1 & 2:1–3; Heb. 4:1–11; Psa. 37:7; Matt. 11:29
1 *What was man's first day?* 2 *How can we enter into God's rest?*

DAY 16

Don't push the river!
ECCLESIASTES 3:1–14

"There is a time for everything, and a season for every activity under heaven." (v. 1: NIV)

We examine yet another principle that can help us cope with stress: *refuse to be obsessed with time*. Notice, I say 'obsessed'. It is right to be concerned about time, but it is not right to be obsessed with it. Do you live life by the clock? Then you are a candidate for stress.

Have you noticed that when film makers want to create tension, they show recurrent shots of a clock relentlessly ticking away? These 'High Noon' tactics are pointless when they are applied to the ordinary issues of everyday life. Nervous glances at a watch will generate tension when you are caught in traffic, but they will not make the traffic move any faster. Fretting and fuming will do nothing to alter the situation. So learn to relax, and do not become intimidated by time.

Some people live life as if they are on a racing track, and set themselves rigid lap times for the things they want to accomplish during the day. A test I read about recently showed how two motorists were given the task of covering a distance of 1700 miles. One was asked to drive as fast as he could without breaking any speed limits; the other was told to drive at a steady, comfortable pace. At the end of their journeys, it was found that the faster driver had consumed ten gallons more petrol and doubled the wear on his tyres by driving at a speed which, in the end, proved to be only 2 mph faster than the other driver! A man said to me in a counselling session when I advised him to slow down: "The trouble is that I'm in a hurry — but God isn't!" Learn the wisdom of letting things develop at their own pace, and follow the maxim that says: "Don't push the river — let it flow."

PRAYER: O Father, save me from being obsessed by time. Help me to see that I have all the time in the world to do what You want me to do. And when I am over-concerned, I am overwrought! Help me, dear Father. Amen.

FURTHER STUDY: Eph. 5:1–21; Col. 4:5; Jas. 4:14
1 *How can we redeem the time?* 2 *To what does James relate this?*

DAY 17

Keeping fit for Jesus!
1 TIMOTHY 4:1–12

"...physical training is of some value, but godliness has value for all things..." (v. 8: NIV)

We spend one last day meditating on the ways by which we can overcome stress in our lives. This final principle is: *engage in as much physical exercise as is necessary.*

One laboratory experiment took ten under-exercised rats, and subjected them repeatedly to a variety of stresses — shock, pain, shrill noises and flashing lights. After a month, every one of them had died through the incessant strain. Another group of rats was taken and given a good deal of exercise until they were in the peak of physical condition. They were then subjected to the same battery of stresses and strains. After a month, not one had died.

More and more Christians are waking up to the fact that God has given us bodies that are designed to *move*, and the more they are exercised, the more effectively they function. Studies on how exercise helps to reduce stress are quite conclusive. Exercise gets rid of harmful chemicals in our bodies, provides a form of abreaction (letting off steam), builds up stamina, counteracts the biochemical effects of stress and reduces the risk of psychological illness. The Bible rarely mentions the need for physical exercise, because people living at that time usually walked everywhere and therefore needed little admonition on the subject. In our world of advanced technology, however, common sense tells us that our bodies need to be exercised, and we should not neglect it. It may not be a spectacular idea, but often God comes to us along some very dusty and lowly roads. We must not despise His coming just because He comes to us along a lowly road.

PRAYER: Lord, help me not to despise this call of Yours to exercise my body. Forgive me that I am such a poor tenant of Your property. From today I determine to do better. For Your own Name's sake. Amen.

FURTHER STUDY: 1 Ki. Ch. 19; 1 Cor. 3:16–17, 6:19
1 *What caused stress in Elijah's life?* 2 *How did God help him?*

DAY 18

When riches take wings
PROVERBS 23:1–8

"Do not wear yourself out to get rich ... Cast but a glance at riches ... for they will surely sprout wings and fly off..."
(vv. 4–5: NIV)

We move on now to consider yet another area of dark threads woven with grace — *financial disaster or material loss*. Some Christians speak scornfully against money. I have heard them quote Scripture in this way: "Money is the root of all evil." They forget that the text actually reads: "The *love* of money is the root of all evil" (1 Tim. 6:10).

Money in itself is not evil. It lends itself to a thousand philanthropies. It feeds the hungry, clothes the naked and succours the destitute, and through it many errands of mercy are performed. Some years ago the Recorder at the Old Bailey made a statement which was taken up by the national press and reported in almost every newspaper. He said, "A couple of pounds very often saves a life — and sometimes a soul." It may be true that money cannot bring happiness but, as somebody said, "It can certainly put our creditors in a better frame of mind." Perhaps nothing hurts more than when life breaks us through a financial reverse, and we experience something of what the writer of the Proverbs describes — 'riches taking wings'.

The first question which we face is this: can we find grace at times of financial failure? We can. I think now as I write of a man I knew some years ago who lost all his assets. Such was his financial reverse that he lost everything — literally everything. Life broke him. He came out of it, however, with a new philosophy that changed his whole attitude toward money. I am sure of this, life will never break him there again. He found grace woven in with the dark threads of the tapestry by the Weaver who loves us with a perfect love. And so, my friend, can you.

PRAYER: O Father, help me over this coming week to settle once and for all my attitude towards this complex problem of money. If it is a weakness, then help me make it a strength. For Jesus' sake. Amen.

FURTHER STUDY: Matt. 6:19–34, 10:29–31; Lk. 12:15
1 *What did Jesus teach about possessions?* 2 *What is to be our priority?*

DAY 19

Transferring the ownership
GENESIS 22:1–19

"... because you ... have not withheld your son, your only son, I will surely bless you..." (vv. 16–17: NIV)

We referred yesterday to the man into whose life were woven dark threads of financial disaster, but who came out of it with a measure of grace that enabled him to say, "Never again will I be broken by material loss." And why? Because he built for himself a Biblical framework which enabled him to see the whole issue of finances from God's point of view.

Here are the steps my friend took in moving from financial bondage to financial freedom, which I recommend to you. (1) *In a definite act of commitment, transfer the ownership of all your possessions to God.* Whether we acknowledge it or not, we do not in reality own our possessions. We are stewards, not proprietors, of the assets which God puts into our hands. My friend told me that, after reading the story of Abraham and his willingness to sacrifice his son, he got alone with God, pictured himself kneeling before God's altar and offered every single one of his possessions to the Lord. He said, "I continued in prayer until every single item I had was laid on God's altar, and when it was over I was a transformed man. That act of dedication became the transformation point in my finances."

If, in reality, we do not own our possessions, then the obvious thing to do is to have the sense to say to God: "Lord, I'm not the owner, but the ower. Teach me how to work out that relationship for as long as I live." When you let go of your possessions and let God have full control, the whole issue of stewardship becomes meaningful. You are handling something on behalf of Another. Money is no longer your master — it becomes instead your messenger.

PRAYER: Father, I'm conscious that, once again, You have Your finger on another sensitive spot. I know I can never be a true disciple until I make this commitment. I do it today — gladly. For Your own dear Name's sake. Amen.

FURTHER STUDY: 1 Ki. Ch. 17; 1 Cor. 4:1–2; Rom. 14:12
1 *What can we learn from the widow at Zarephath?* 2 *What is the characteristic of a steward?*

DAY 20
"Hitched to a plough"
COLOSSIANS 3:1–17

"Set your minds on things above, not on earthly things." (v. 2: NIV)

We continue looking at the steps we can take in order to overcome financial disaster and find grace at this place of darkness.

(2) *Streamline your life toward the purposes of God's Kingdom.* Livingstone once said, "I will place no value on anything that I have or possess, except in relation to the Kingdom of Christ. If anything I have will advance that Kingdom, it shall be given or kept, whichever will best promote the glory of Him to whom I owe all my hopes, both for time and eternity." Another great missionary said, "That first sentence of Livingstone's should become the life motto of every Christian. Each Christian should repeat this slowly to himself every day: *I will place no value on anything I have or possess, except in relation to the Kingdom of Christ.*" If it advances the Kingdom, it has value — it can stay. If it is useless to the Kingdom, it is valueless — it must be made useful, or go.

John Wanamaker, a fine Christian businessman, visited China many years ago to see if the donations he had made to missionary work were being used to their best advantage. One day he came to a village where there was a beautiful church, and in a nearby field, he caught sight of a young man yoked together with an ox, ploughing a field. He went over and asked what was the purpose of this strange yoking. An old man who was driving the plough said, "When we were trying to build the church, my son and I had no money to give, and my son said, 'Let us sell one of our two oxen and I will take its yoke.' We did so and gave the money to the chapel." Wanamaker wept!

PRAYER: Father, I feel like weeping too when I consider how little of my life is streamlined for Kingdom purposes. Help me to be willing to be hitched to a plough and know the joy of sacrifice. For Jesus' sake. Amen.

FURTHER STUDY: Jas. 4:8–17; Rom. 14:8; Psa. 24:1; Hag. 2:8
1 *How should we approach life?* 2 *Is your value system Biblical?*

DAY 21
Riches or poverty — so what?
PHILIPPIANS 4:4–13

"I know what it is to be in need, and I know what it is to have plenty. I have learned the secret of being content in any ... situation..." (v. 12: NIV)

We are meditating on the steps we should take to rebuild our lives following a financial collapse: (3) *Recognise that you are only free when you are free to use either poverty or plenty.*

There are two ways in which men and women try to defend themselves against financial disaster. One is by saving as much as possible in an attempt to avert it. The other is by renouncing money or material things entirely in order to be free from their clutches. Both methods have disadvantages. The first, because it can cause miserliness and anxiety, and tends to make a person as metallic as the coins they seek to amass. The second, because it seeks to get rid of the difficulty by washing one's hands of it entirely. In each case, there is a bondage — one is a bondage to material things, the other a bondage to poverty. The man who is free to use plenty *only* is bound by that, while the man who is free to use poverty *only* is also bound. They are both bound. But the person who, like Paul, in the text before us today, has "learned the secret of being content ... whether living in plenty or in want" is free — really free.

While waiting for a train in India, a missionary got into conversation with a high-caste Indian. "Are you travelling on the next train?" the missionary asked. "No," he replied, "that train has only third class carriages. It's all right for you, because you are a Christian. Third class doesn't degrade you and first class doesn't exalt you. You are above these distinctions, but I have to observe them." *Lifted above all distinctions.* It's enough to make you throw your hat in the air!

PRAYER: O Father, what a way to live — lifted above all distinctions. Plenty doesn't entangle my spirit, and poverty doesn't break it. No matter how I have lived in the past — this is how I want to live in the future. Help me, dear Lord. Amen.

FURTHER STUDY: Jas. 2:1–10, 5:1–8
1 *Where does favouritism come from?* 2 *What does James say about selfish living?*

DAY 22

A need or a want?
PHILIPPIANS 4:14–23

"And my God will meet all your needs according to his glorious riches in Christ Jesus." (v. 19: NIV)

Today we look at yet another step that will help us overcome financial disaster: (4) *Learn to differentiate between a need and a want.* Your needs are important, but not your wants. God has promised to supply all your needs, but not all your wants.

What are our needs? Someone defined it like this: "We need as much as will make us physically, mentally and spiritually fit for the purposes of the Kingdom of God. Anything beyond that belongs to other people's needs." If this is true, then how do we decide what belongs to our needs? No one can decide that for you; it must be worked out between you and God. Go over your life in God's presence and see what belongs to your needs, and what belongs to your wants. Let the Holy Spirit sensitise your conscience so that you can distinguish the difference.

A fisherman tells this story: "Yesterday I was on the lake. I pulled in my oars and let my boat drift. As I looked at the surrounding water, I could see no drift at all. Only as I looked at the fixed point of the shore line could I see how far I was drifting." It is a parable! If you look around you to see what others are doing and merely follow, you will have no sense of drift. It is only as you fix your eyes on Christ, and watch for His approval, that you will know whether you are staying on God's course — or drifting away from it. One more thing: keep your needs strictly to needs, not luxuries disguised as needs. If you eat more than you need, you clog up your system. It is the same with other things. Needs contribute: luxuries choke.

PRAYER: Gracious Father, bring me under the sway of Your creative Spirit. Sensitise my inner being so that I might hear Your voice when I am about to go off course. This I ask for Your own dear Name's sake. Amen.

FURTHER STUDY: Ex. Ch. 16; Psa. 23:5, 33:18–19, 37:25
1 *How did God supply the needs of the Israelites?* 2 *List some of the needs God has supplied in your life.*

DAY 23

Promises! Promises!
PROVERBS 20:1–22

"... 'It's no good!' says the buyer; then off he goes and boasts about his purchase." (v. 14: NIV)

We continue following the steps that help us find grace woven into the fabric of financial disaster: (5) *Ask God to help you resist the powerful pressures of this modern-day consumer society.*

I once listened to a sermon in which the preacher likened Satan's conversation with Eve in the Garden of Eden with the subtle tactics of modern advertising. The main point he made was that if Eve could become discontent with all she had in that lush garden called Paradise, there is little hope for us unless we identify and reject modern methods of alluring advertising. What exactly is alluring advertising? One definition puts it like this: "Alluring advertising is a carefully planned appeal to our human weakness, which is designed to make us discontented with what we have so that we can rationalise buying things we know we do not need and should not have."

Not all advertising, of course, falls into this category, but much of it does. Charles Swindoll, an American author, claims that some advertising is not just alluring, but definitely demonic. I agree. He says that he and his family have developed a simple technique to overrule television commercials that attempt to convince us that we need a certain product in order to be happy. He describes it like this: "Every time we feel a persuasive tug from a television commercial, we simply shout at the top of our voices: 'Who do you think you're kidding!'" He claims it really works. God expects us to discipline ourselves in relation to many things, and not the least in the discipline of spiritual 'sales resistance'.

PRAYER: Father, help me, I pray, to see right through the alluring advertising of today's world, and develop within me the wisdom and strength to build up a strong spiritual 'sales resistance'. For Your honour and glory I ask it. Amen.

FURTHER STUDY: 1 Jn. 2:12–17; Gen. 3:6; Jas. 1:13–16
1 *What are the three avenues which advertising exploits?* 2 *What is John's admonition?*

DAY 24

"Be a generous person"
1 TIMOTHY 6:6–19

"Command them ... to be generous and willing to share. In this way they will lay up treasure for themselves ..."
(vv. 18–19: NIV)

We have been discussing during the past week the steps we need to take to receive grace in those areas where financial disaster is woven into our lives. The friend I previously referred to claims that the principles we have been focusing on helped him to develop such spiritual strength and wisdom in relation to money that he was confident that, with God's help, financial disaster would never again represent dark threads.

The sixth and final principle he used, and which we need to practise too, is this: (6) *Become a generous person*. Look again at the text at the top of this page. It is so clear that it hardly needs any explanation. Woven through the fabric of these verses, as well as in many others in the New Testament, is the thought: give, give, give, give, give. When you have money, don't hoard it, release it. Let generosity become your trademark. This is not to say that you have to give all your money away, but give as much as you can, and as much as you believe God would have you give. Jesus once said, "If your Eye is generous, the whole of your body will be illumined" (Moffatt translation).

What does this mean? If your Eye — your outlook on life, your whole way of looking at things and people — is generous, then your whole personality is illumined, lit up. Jesus had little to give in terms of finances, but He was generous toward all — the sick, the needy, the maimed, the sinful and the unlovely. His whole personality was full of light. So be like Jesus — begin to see everybody and everything with a generous Eye. Don't be a mean person. One of the greatest definitions of Christianity I have ever heard is simply this: "Give, give, give, give, give …"

PRAYER: Lord Jesus, help me this day and every day of my life from now on, to make generosity the basis of all my dealings with people. Make me the channel and not the dead end of all Your generosity to me. For Your dear Name's sake. Amen.

FURTHER STUDY: Lk. 21:1–4, 6:38; Eccl. 11:1; Acts 4:32–35; Matt. 5:42
1 *What did Jesus teach about giving?* 2 *How did the early Church work this out?*

DAY 25

Transformed!
PSALM 32:1–11

"Blessed is he whose transgressions are forgiven, whose sins are covered." (v. 1: NIV)

Finally we ask ourselves — can the dark threads be apparent rather than real? Can we think dark threads are woven where there are none? I think the answer is yes and would suggest that one area where this is particularly distressing for Christians is *the memory of some deeply grievous sin*.

I am not thinking so much of those who have committed sin and have not come to Christ for forgiveness, but of those who, though they have been forgiven by God, are unable to forgive themselves. A man came to me recently at the end of a meeting at which I had spoken, and told me the details of a particularly horrendous sin in which he had been involved. He said, "I know God has forgiven me, but the memory of what I have done is constantly with me. It is quietly driving me insane."

This brought to mind a story I heard many years ago of a father who taught his son to drive a nail into a board every time he did something wrong, and then to pull out the nail after he had confessed the wrong and had been forgiven. Every time this happened, the boy would say triumphantly, "Hurray! The nails are gone!" "Yes," his father would say, "but always remember that the marks made by the nails are still in the wood." The message I want you to get hold of and build into your life in these last few days is this: the Carpenter of Nazareth can not only pull out the nails, but so varnish and beautify the wood that the marks become, not a contradiction, but a contribution.

PRAYER: Lord Jesus Christ, You who once were known as a carpenter's son, take the stains and blemishes of my past and work through them so that they contribute, rather than contradict. For Your own dear Name's sake. Amen.

FURTHER STUDY: 1 Jn. Ch. 1; Psa. 103:3; Acts 5:31; Eph. 1:7
1 *How can we know full forgiveness?* 2 *Why not ask for it today?*

DAY 26

Grace — greater than all our sin!
ROMANS 5:12–21

"...where sin abounded, grace did much more abound." (v. 20)

We are meditating, in these last few days, on how to recover from the effects of the memory of some deeply grievous sin. By that we mean a sin which God has forgiven but which, for some reason, still burns in our memory. What principles can we use to cope with this distressing situation?

The first principle is this: *realise that God can do more with sin than just forgive it.* I heard an elderly minister make that statement many years ago, when I was a young Christian, and at first I resisted it — as you may do at this moment. I said to myself: "How can God *use* sin? Surely it is His one intolerance?" Then, after pondering for a while, I saw what he meant. God uses our sin, not by encouraging us to gloat over it, but by using it to motivate our will toward greater spiritual achievement, to quicken our compassion toward sinners and to show God's tender heart for the fallen.

We must be careful, of course, that we do not fall into the error which Paul refers to in Romans 6:1–2:"Shall we continue in sin, that grace may abound? God forbid!" (AV). If we sin in order that God may use it, then our motive is all wrong and we fall foul of the eternal purposes. If, however, we commit sin, but then take it to God in confession — *really* take it to Him — then He will not only forgive it, but make something of it. Is this too difficult for you to conceive? Then I point you to the cross. The cross was the foulest deed mankind ever committed; yet God used it to become the fulcrum of His redemption. It was our nadir — our lowest point — but it was God's zenith. Hallelujah.

PRAYER: O Father, I am so relieved to know that You take even my sins and make them contribute to Your purposes. Grace turns all my bad into good, all my good into better and all my better into the best. Hallelujah!

FURTHER STUDY: Heb. 10:1–22; Isa. 43:25, 44:22, 55:7
1 *What will God not remember any more?* 2 *What is the "full assurance" we can have?*

DAY 27 — Why do I do these things?
1 JOHN 1:1–10

"If we confess our sins, he is faithful and just and will forgive us our sins and purify us from all unrighteousness." (v. 9: NIV)

We continue meditating on the principles that enable us to recover from the persistence of the memory of some dark and grievous sin. A second principle is this: *understand the major reason why you tend to brood on the past*. People who brood on the past, and keep the memory of their sin alive, do so for several reasons: (1) they are not sure that God has forgiven them; (2) they are in the grip of spiritual pride; and (3) they have not forgiven themselves.

Let's take them one by one: (1) *They are not sure that God has forgiven them*. If you have this kind of doubt, then you must see that the doubt is really a *denial*. It is taking a verse, like the one before us today, and flinging it back into God's face, saying, "I don't believe it." You see, if you don't accept God's forgiveness, you will try to make your own atonement — in feelings of guilt and self-debasement. Once you confess your sin, then, as far as God is concerned, that's the end of it. Believe that — and act upon it. It's the Gospel truth!

(2) *They are in the grip of spiritual pride.* You could be saying to yourself, at some deep level of your mental and emotional life: how could *I* have ever done a thing like that? (Note the stress on the 'I'.) What this really amounts to is that you have too high an opinion of yourself. And that's about as bad as too low an opinion of yourself. (3) *They have not forgiven themselves.* It might help to stand in front of a mirror with your Bible open at the verse at the top of this page, reassure yourself that God has forgiven you, and say to yourself, by name: " _____ God has forgiven you — *now I forgive you too!*"

PRAYER: Gracious Father, although I understand many things, I fail so often to understand myself. Teach me more of what goes on deep inside me, so that, being more self-aware, I may become more God-aware. For Your own dear Name's sake. Amen.

FURTHER STUDY: Psa. 51:1–19; Eph. 4:32; Col. 3:13; Mk. 12:33
1 *Why can we forgive ourselves?* 2 *Forgive yourself today.*

DAY 28

Remembering to forget
PHILIPPIANS 3:1–14

"...forgetting what lies behind and straining forward to what lies ahead, I press on toward the goal..." (vv. 13–14: RSV)

We examine one more principle in relation to this highly important matter of recovering from the brokenness caused by the memory of some dark and grievous sin: *forget the matter by reversing the process of remembering.* Puzzled? Then let me explain. Memory works like this: one revives an image of some past event (or sin), holds it in the mind for a certain length of time, and then this process is repeated again and again until it is locked into the memory for good. Now begin to reverse that process. *Don't* revive the image. The matter has been forgiven by God, so don't let your mind focus on it. When it rises to the surface by itself, as it will, turn the mind away from it immediately.

Have in your mind a few interesting themes 'on call' — a favourite Bible character, or a text which has special meaning. We are told that the mind, like nature, abhors a vacuum — so think of another and more profitable theme. I know a Christian man, once involved in one of the deepest sins imaginable, who has learned to blot out unwanted memories the moment they rise to the surface by focusing his thoughts on the Cross. It does not matter what the substitute image is, so long as it is wholesome and can thrust the unwanted memory from your attention.

Another thing you can do when the memory of your sin returns — even if it is only for a moment — is to turn your mind to prayer. Don't pray about the sin itself — that will keep it in the memory — but pray that God will build into you love, forgiveness, peace and poise. Images that are consciously rejected will rise less and less in your mind. When they do occur, they will occur only as *fact*: the emotions will no longer register a sense of burning shame.

PRAYER: O my Father, how can I cease thanking You for the answers You give — they are so right. Everything within me says so. Now help me to put the things I am learning into practice. Amen.

FURTHER STUDY: 2 Sam. 12:1–14; Mk. 2:5; Col. 2:13; Heb. 8:12
1 *What was Nathan's message to David?* 2 *What does God do besides forgive?*